Rain Forests
Around the World

by Jeanne Baca Schulte

PEARSON

Glenview, Illinois • Boston, Massachusetts
Chandler, Arizona • Upper Saddle River, New Jersey

A tropical rain forest

You are walking through a thick forest. It is very hot. It won't stop raining. Everything is wet—even the air. You hear singing birds and other animals. When you look up, you can see only the tops of tall trees. Where are you?

You are in a tropical rain forest!

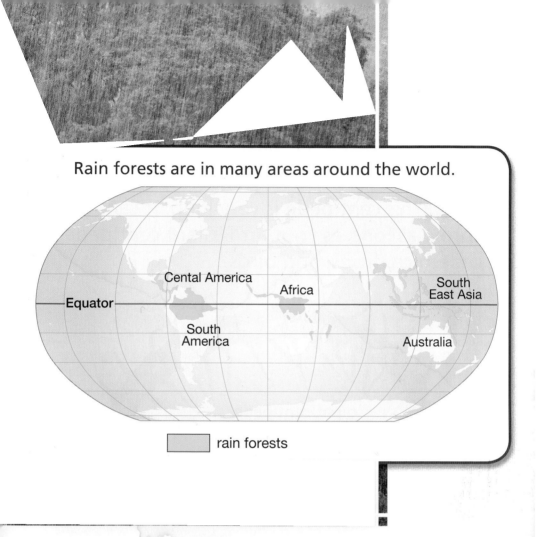

Rain forests are in many areas around the world.

Cental America

Africa

South East Asia

Equator

South America

Australia

rain forests

Where Are Tropical Rain Forests?

Tropical rain forests are near the Equator. The Equator is a line around Earth. We cannot see this line. In this area, the weather is hot and wet.

Rain forests cover about six percent of Earth. Millions of plants and animals live in rain forests. You can find different kinds in each area.

Rain Forests in South America

The Amazon is the biggest rain forest in the world. It is full of insects!

Giant centipedes (SEN tuh peeds) live there. A centipede is a long bug with many legs. This centipede is very long. It can grow as long as your arm. Giant centipedes eat mice, frogs, and birds.

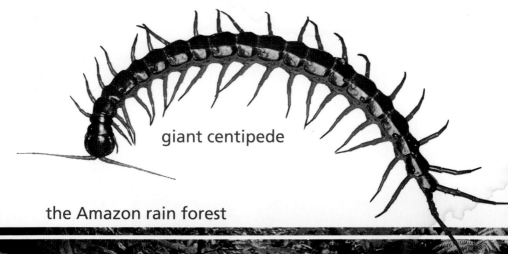

giant centipede

the Amazon rain forest

scales

green mamba snake

African grey parrot

Rain Forests in Africa

In African rain forests, parrots live in the trees. The African grey parrot is very smart. It can **repeat** almost any sound it hears.

Snakes live in trees too. The green mamba snake has scales to help it hold the branches. It will attack when it is in danger. Its **venom** is very dangerous.

---

repeat: to say again
venom: poison that animals use to attack other animals

5

Rain Forests in Southeast Asia

In Southeast Asia, mangrove trees grow on shores. The tall roots keep the trees straight.

The mud skipper is a fish that lives around the mangroves. It is the only fish that lives on water and on land. Some can even climb trees!

---

shores: where land meets the ocean

Mangrove trees have tall roots.

mud skipper

roots

A tree kangaroo can jump down from more than 30 feet.

Rain Forests in Australia

In Australia, the tree kangaroo jumps from tree to tree. It looks like a bear. Tree kangaroos have short back legs and strong front arms. They climb and hop through the trees.

cocoa beans

cashew nuts

bananas

Over half of all plants and animals live in rain forests. The plants and animals depend on each other to survive.

People depend on rain forests too. We use medicines made from their plants. We eat food from rain forests, like bananas, cocoa, and nuts.

Scientists learn new rain forest secrets every day. What do you think they will learn next?

---

depend: need something in order to survive